I Can Be Responsible

Doing the Right Thing

Written by Jenette Donovan Guntly
Illustrated by Priscilla Burris

GARETH STEVENS
GS
PUBLISHING
A World Almanac Education Group Company

Please visit our web site at: www.garethstevens.com
For a free color catalog describing Gareth Stevens Publishing's list of high-quality books
and multimedia programs, call 1-800-542-2595 (USA) or 1-800-387-3178 (Canada).
Gareth Stevens Publishing's fax: (414) 332-3567.

Library of Congress Cataloging-in-Publication Data

Guntly, Jenette Donovan.
    (You can count on me)
    I can be responsible / written by Jenette Donovan Guntly; illustrated by Priscilla Burris.
        p. cm. — (Doing the right thing)
    ISBN 0-8368-4245-6 (lib. bdg.)
    1. Responsibility—Juvenile literature. I. Burris, Priscilla. II. Title.
    BJ1451.G77   2004
    179'.9—dc22   2004045298

This North American edition first published in 2005 by
Gareth Stevens Publishing
A World Almanac Education Group Company
330 West Olive Street, Suite 100
Milwaukee, WI 53212 USA

This edition copyright © 2005 by Gareth Stevens, Inc. Original edition copyright © 2002 by Creative Teaching Press, Inc.,
P.O. Box 2723, Huntington Beach, CA 92647-0723. First published in the United States in 2002 as *You Can Count on Me:
Learning about Responsibility* by Creative Teaching Press, Inc. Original text copyright © 2002 by Regina G. Burch.

Illustrator: Priscilla Burris
Gareth Stevens designer: Kami M. Koenig

Printed in the United States of America

1 2 3 4 5 6 7 8 9 08 07 06 05 04

I can be responsible!

I brush my teeth all by myself.

I tuck my blankets tight.

I do my best in every class.

I do my homework right.

I bring books back when they are due.

I share with all my friends.

I try to help my neighbors out.

I clean up odds and ends.

I help keep all my laundry clean.

I put my clothes away.

I take good care of my best friend.

I feed my fish each day.

I know that when my work is done,
I am free to have some fun.